Everyday History

Toys and Games

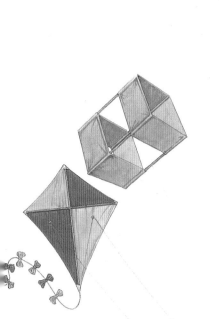

Philip Steele

W
FRANKLIN WATTS
A Division of Grolier Publishing
NEW YORK • LONDON • HONG KONG • SYDNEY
DANBURY, CONNECTICUT

Photographs:
4 Martin Dohrn/Bruce Coleman, 5 Bridgeman Art Library, 6
Werner Forman Archive, 7 top and bottom Ronald
Sheridan/Ancient Art & Architecture Collection Ltd, 8 top
Bridgeman Art Library,
8 bottom E.T. Archive, 10 Bridgeman Art Library,
11 Bridgeman Art Library, 12 Bridgeman Art Library, 13 bottom
Museum of Childhood Edinburgh,
14 Bridgeman Art Library, 15 Museum of Childhood Edinburgh, 17
Bridgeman Art Library, 18 Bridgeman Art Library, 19 top
Museum of Childhood Edinburgh, 19 bottom E.T. Archive, 20 &
21 Bridgeman Art Library, 22 Museum of Childhood Edinburgh,
23 top Bridgeman Art Library, 23 bottom Museum of Childhood
Bethnal Green/British Museum, 24 Last Resort Picture Library,
28 David Stoecklein/The Stock Market

Acknowledgements
Franklin Watts wishes to thank the following
for their kind permission to use their material:
Disney Enterprises, Humbrol/Airfix, Lego, Mattel/Barbie, Sony

Planning and production by Discovery Books Limited
Editors: Gianna Williams, Claire Berridge
Design: Ian Winton
Art Director: Robert Walster
Illustrators: Stefan Chabluk, John James,
Joanna Williams

First published in 1999 by Franklin Watts

First American edition 1999 by Franklin Watts/Children's Press
A Division of Grolier Publishing
90 Sherman Turnpike
Danbury, CT 06816

Library of Congress Cataloging-in-Publication Data
Steele, Philip.
        Toys and Games / Philip Steele. -- 1st American ed.
            p.   cm. -- (Everyday History)
        Includes bibliographical references and index.
        Summary: Details various types of toys from ancient times
to the present day, including dolls, puppets, clockwork, teddy
bears, and electronic games.
        ISBN 0-531-14548-4 (hbk)
                0-531-15402-5 (pbk)
        1. Toys--History--Juvenile literature. 2. Games--History--
Juvenile literature. [1. Toys--History.] I. Title. II. Series.
NK9509.S88 2000
394'.3--dc21   99-12048
                                                                      CIP

GROLIER
PUBLISHING

Contents

Come Out to Play!

Watch how young animals play. Kittens chase each other around and pounce upon their mother's tail. They copy the mother cat's movements. Playing isn't just fun for them. It helps them learn how to behave and survive.

Hagehai boys from New Guinea practice archery. They will have to find their own food when they are 8 years old.

The First Toys

The children of the first humans played for the same sorts of reasons. They probably copied their parents, too, hunting with toy spears made from sticks. They must have raced each other and thrown stones, or made mud pies just as small children do today.

The Stone Age

Stone Age children, living more than 10,000 years ago, may have played with dolls made from feathers, fur, sticks, or clay. They probably made gourds into rattles and invented games with shells, pebbles, or seeds.

Few toys have survived from prehistoric times. Wood has rotted away and clay has turned to dust. Little stone figures have survived, but these were probably good luck charms.

The Game of Kings

This board game is one of the oldest ones we know about. It was played by Sumerian princes in the ancient city of Ur, about 4,500 years ago.

Few Sumerians could have afforded such fine sets. They probably just moved pebbles over squares scratched out in the dust.

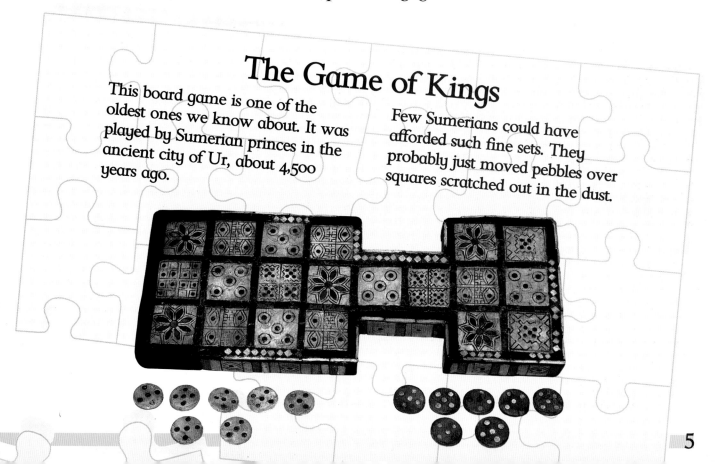

In Ancient Times

About 4,000 years ago, ancient Egyptian children wrestled in the sand and swam in the River Nile. They had to be careful of the crocodiles that lived in the river.

Egyptians playing a board game called senet.

This spinning disc was made in ancient Egypt more than 4,000 years ago. When it was spun, the dogs chased the gazelles around and around.

They played with spinning tops and with brightly colored balls made of rags or papyrus, a type of reed. They had toy animals, too.

Games in Ancient Greece

In Europe, children were already playing with dolls, balls, spinning tops, and rattles thousands of years ago. In ancient Greece, about 2,500 years ago, children used to play with rag dolls and with funny clay models of people riding geese or donkeys. They also played with yo-yos.

When Greek children turned 12, they offered their old toys to the gods to show that they were now grown up.

Roman Times

About 2,000 years ago, Roman toddlers were shaking clay animals to hear the rattling pebbles inside.

Older children played with dolls and marbles. The Romans loved playing all kinds of board games. A favorite one with children was called three-stones and was a bit like tic-tac-toe.

This puppet is from the Roman province of Gaul, now modern France.

▼ Toy chariots were popular in Roman times.

In the Middle Ages

Roman rule came to an end in Europe over 1,500 years ago. The five hundred years that followed are known as the Middle Ages. Wars and plagues were common. Games helped people to enjoy themselves in these troubled times.

War games

In northern Europe, young Vikings had already learned to play a boardgame called *hnefatafl*. Later in the Middle Ages, knights and ladies taught their children how to play draughts, chess or a kind of backgammon.

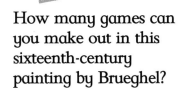

How many games can you make out in this sixteenth-century painting by Brueghel?

▼ Europeans playing chess in the fourteenth century.

An easier game was called nine-men's-morris. Many boardgames were rather like battles, played out for fun.

Medieval toys

Most children preferred playing with toy soldiers. These lead-weighted figures were jiggled on cords, in mock battle. Boys bowled hoops along the muddy streets. When windmills were first built in Europe, children were soon running around with whirling toy windmills on sticks.

Football fans

Children had little time to play in the Middle Ages. In towns, some boys were sent to learn a trade. These apprentices liked to play football in the streets. A pig's bladder was used for a ball, and there weren't really any rules. In fact, the sport became so rough that King Edward II of England had it banned in 1314.

Ride a Rocking Horse

Children today like to play with toy cars and trucks. In the days when people traveled by horse and cart, every child wanted to play with wooden horses, or rocking horses. They are still popular today.

Hobbyhorses

A hobbyhorse is a simple pole with a carved horse's head on one end. It is often decorated with ribbons. Hobbyhorses were first made thousands of years ago, but were particularly popular from the Middle Ages until the 1800s.

This little girl in the nineteenth century has a toy whip for her wheeled horse.

Make a Hobbyhorse

You will need a stick, pole, or bamboo cane about the same height as you.

1. Draw a horse's head and neck onto stiff cardboard and cut it out. Paint it in bright colors and leave it to dry.

2. Cut holes along the horse's mane and thread them with colored ribbons.

3. Use clear tape to stick one side of the horse's neck to the pole or stick.

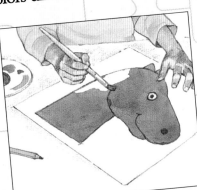

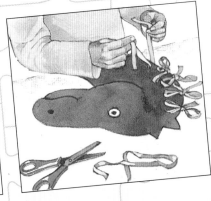

Horses with Wheels

From the 1500s onward, wheeled horses were children's favorites. Some had wheels hidden in their hooves; others were on wheeled platforms. The smaller of these were for toddlers to pull and push. The bigger ones were for riding.

Rocking Horses

Wooden rocking horses became popular in the 1600s. Some had toy pistols in holsters. At first the sides of the rocking horses were boat-shaped, with solid rockers.

The horses became more realistic in the 1700s and 1800s, with finely curved rockers. About 1900, a safer type of rocking horse became popular. It was mounted on wooden beams.

A nineteenth-century rocking horse.

Dolls and Dollhouses

In the 1500s, many Europeans crossed the Atlantic Ocean to settle in the Americas. They took dolls with them, and these were among the first goods to be traded with the Native American peoples who lived there. Many of the settlers were soon making their own dolls, carved from pinewood.

Workshops

Back in Europe, during the 1600s, more and more dolls began to be made in special workshops. The German city of Nuremberg became famous for its toy makers and toy fairs. Beautiful dollhouses were made there, and were complete in every detail.

This dollhouse was made in 1740. It gives us a very good idea of how wealthy people lived in those days.

Handmade Dolls

Dolls have always been popular in every part of the world. If you couldn't afford to buy one, you made the doll yourself. These African-American dolls were handmade early in the twentieth century.

Dutch Dollhouses

Some of the finest dollhouses of all were made in the Netherlands. They were probably far too precious to play with! Today most of these "cabinet houses" are in museums.

By the 1700s and 1800s, dolls were more lifelike than ever. They were now made from all sorts of materials, such as papier mâché, wax, china, stuffed cloth, and rubber. Cheap wooden dolls were sold far and wide by traveling peddlers.

These Bru dolls were made in France about 120 years ago. Their heads are made of bisque, a type of porcelain.

Puppets and Theaters

Do you remember the story of Pinocchio? It was written over a hundred years ago, and it is about an Italian puppet maker and his magical creation, whose wooden nose grew longer every time he lied. Many puppets were made in Italy.

Puppet Plays

Puppets have been popular for thousands of years. In Britain, in the 1600s, both children and adults used to watch puppet plays. These were often based on old folk tales, such as *Dick Whittington*.

Moving Shadows

These shadow puppets are from the island of Java, in Southeast Asia. They were moved by wires, behind a cotton screen. Lit by a lantern at the rear, their shadows moved across the screen like characters in a film. The puppets acted out ancient stories of heroes, villains, gods, and goddesses.

Punch and Judy

In the early 1900s, Punch and Judy shows were often held in British town squares and at the seaside. These glove puppets were based on funny characters from the Italian theater. Children liked to play with their own puppets, too, and make up their own shows.

Toy Theaters

In the 1800s toy theaters were bought by adults, as souvenirs of plays they had seen. Soon toy theaters were being made for children. These featured pantomimes such as *Jack and the Beanstalk*.

Out and About

Many outdoor games have changed little in hundreds of years. Follow the leader, seesaw, king of the castle, and hopscotch have always been favorites. In the 1700s many children liked to make toy parachutes from their handkerchiefs.

Make a Toy Parachute

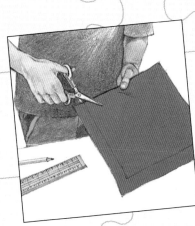

1. You will need to cut a piece of tissue paper about 10 in (25 cm) square and four lengths of cotton thread 6 in (15 cm) long.

2. Attach a thread to each corner of the square, using tape.

3. Tie the ends of the threads around two paper clips — and drop your parachute out of a window.

Chinese Kites

Kites were invented in China about 1,700 years ago. Many old Chinese kites were shaped like beautiful birds or butterflies. Paper kites were soon being made by children all over Asia. By the 1300s, kites had reached Europe.

During the 1700s and 1800s, kites became very popular in Europe and America. Most of these were simple diamond shapes made of light cloth. They had long tails tied with ribbons and bows. Modern kites come in all shapes, sizes, and materials.

By the Seaside

In the 1800s, people began to go to the seaside on vacation. They often traveled there on the new railways. Children would play with pails and shovels, just like today. Toy sailing boats were popular, and long hours were often spent trying to catch small fish and crabs with nets.

A boy and his boat painted in the late nineteenth century.

A Victorian Christmas

The Victorian period is named after the days when Queen Victoria ruled the British Empire in the 1800s. It was in this period that the German custom of putting up a Christmas tree, covered in candles, began to spread to other lands. What presents might Victorian children expect to play with on Christmas morning?

Victorian Toys

There were wooden skittles and skipping ropes. There were spinning tops, which could be whipped to a flying start with a cord. Hoops were more popular than ever. They were bowled along with small sticks. Children held hoop races and set up difficult courses to follow, in a game called turnpikes.

Decorations were hung on the Christmas tree, with the presents placed underneath.

There were tin drums, trumpets, tin soldiers, and forts. There were jack-in-the-boxes and jumping jacks, too. These were figures whose arms and legs flew out when you pulled a string.

This Noah's ark, with a full set of animals, was made in Germany in the 1800s.

Building Blocks

Simple blocks were made for toddlers, decorated with pictures or letters. Complicated building bricks were made for older children, and these could be used to make impressive railway stations, palaces, or town halls.

A nineteenth-century board game.

Around the Table

The Victorians loved to play board games and cards, although gambling was disapproved of. Games and puzzles, such as the first jigsaws, were often expected to be educational. For example, children would put together a map of the world.

Tin and Clockwork

During the 1800s, inexpensive toys began to be made on a large scale. In France, toys were now being made from tinplate — thin sheets of iron coated with tin. These were pressed and cut into shape.

Tin Cans

Tin cans were also collected and re-used to make toys. By the 1880s, factories in the United States were supplying the world with vast numbers of tin toys.

Penny Toys

The tin toys of the 1900s are known as penny toys. They didn't each cost a penny, but they were cheap enough to buy with a bit of pocket money.

Moving Clockwork

Simple clockwork and steel springs that could be wound up with a key now made it possible for children to have toy monkeys, drummer boys, paddle steamers, trains, and model merry-go-rounds that actually moved. Clockwork toys remained popular into the 1950s.

Planes, Trains, and Automobiles

The 1900s were a time of great changes. Children loved to see the new cars, buses, and delivery vans that were appearing on city streets.

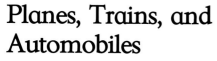

Powerful new steamers crossed the oceans, and soon the skies too were filled with the first planes and airships. Models of all these soon became some of the most popular toys of all.

Teddy, Mickey, and Company

In 1903, a new toy appeared in the stores – the teddy bear. Toy bears had been made for many years, but these had mostly stood on all fours. Teddy bears were different, because they sat, or stood on two legs. They looked more like babies and were easier to cuddle.

This teddy bear is one of the oldest in existence today. It was made in 1907.

Why Teddy?

Teddy bears are probably named after Theodore "Teddy" Roosevelt, a U.S. president who liked to go bear hunting. One day in 1902, he spared a little brown bear cub. The incident was made into a newspaper cartoon. A New York shopkeeper called Morris Michtom saw this picture and made a "Teddy" bear for sale.

Famous Teddies

In no time at all, German toy factories were shipping out nearly a million new teddy bears a year. Teddies became nursery favorites all over the world and remain so to this day. They have been the heroes of many famous children's stories, such as *Winnie the Pooh* and *Paddington Bear*.

Stuffed Animals

All sorts of stuffed animals could soon be found alongside teddy bears. Pandas were very popular in the 1930s, when these animals first appeared in zoos in the United States and Europe.

Toys and Cartoons

In 1928 another famous name was born when the American filmmaker Walt Disney created a cartoon character named Mickey Mouse.

A 1930s Mickey Mouse doll.

Mickey soon appeared in the form of a popular toy. Today the selling of toys is closely linked to new films and television programs.

Film stars such as Shirley Temple were also popular dolls in the 1930s.

Make and Do

Children arranged these colored marbles into shapes.

hat would an 11-year-old boy want for his birthday in the 1930s? Probably a chemistry set or a working steam engine. He would enjoy making things stink and fizz and hiss. In those days, most girls were expected not to be interested in such things! They might have been given a needlework set instead, with bands of colored silk threads. Modeling clays, such as Play-Doh, were popular with both boys and girls.

Meccano Magic

Kits for making working models were very popular from the 1920s until the 1960s. With Meccano, made in England, small metal bars, wheels, and plates could be bolted together to make cranes, tractors, and other machines that really worked.

Building Bricks

Model buildings and other structures could be made from interlocking bricks. These were made of wood, and then of rubber or an early type of plastic called Bakelite. The Danish company Lego introduced plastic bricks in 1949.

Lego kits from the 1940s and 1950s.

Super Models

Children were already making their own model ships and aircraft, but by the 1950s kits were being mass-produced on a large scale. This made it much easier to put the models together. Planes made of light balsa wood could be powered by rubber bands or little motors.

Plastic model kits have been popular since the 1950s.

Fantastic Plastic

From the 1950s onward, more and more toys were made of the new plastics that were being produced. These were tough, light, and cheap. All kinds of toys that had once been made of wood or metal were now produced in plastic, from yo-yos to electric trains.

Hula Hoops

In 1958, a new plastic hoop was produced in the United States. It was named the hula hoop, after a Hawaiian dance called the hula. The inventors of the hula hoop sold 20 million of them in the first six months!

Battery Power

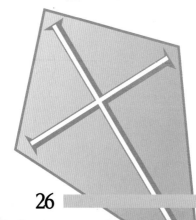

Wind-up toys were still made, but more toys were now powered by batteries. These were fitted into space rockets or ray guns with flashing lights, into musical keyboards or toy cars. Starting in the 1970s, cars run by remote control became popular.

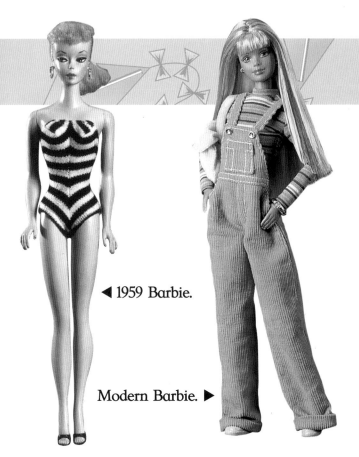

◄ 1959 Barbie.

Modern Barbie. ▶

▲ Barbie was launched in New York in 1959. How different does she look today?

Plastic Dolls

Plastics were also good materials for making dolls. During the 1960s, even young girls became interested in fashion. Plastic dolls, such as the American Barbie and Ken, or the British Sindy, came with a costume for every occasion. G.I. Joe was a doll for boys. These moving figures were dressed as soldiers or pilots and were fully armed.

▼ Plastic figures from films, such as *Star Wars*, which came out in 1977, took the place of metal soldiers and cowboys.

STAR WARS™

HAN SOLO'S™
MILLENNIUM FALCON™

WORKING FEATURES
PIECES FONCTIONNANT
BEWEGLICHE TEILE

WITH LIGHTS
AVEC LUMIERES
MIT BELEUCHTUNG

MODEL KIT
MODELE REDUIT
MODELLBAUSATZ

AIRFIX

Cybergames

I n the 1970s and 1980s, there were all kinds of exciting new developments in the world of computers and videos. The first simple video game, a kind of tennis played on screen, was invented in the United States in 1972.

Today's computer monsters.

Home Computers

In the 1980s, personal computers became common in many homes. New computer games were produced. Some were based on traditional board games, such as chess. Others were fantasy adventures, in which children could drive spacecraft, attack castles, or fight monsters.

A Sony PlayStation game.

Boards and Blades

If you were tired of games in the electronic world, the 1990s offered all kinds of things to do outdoors, too. The old metal roller skates, invented in the 1800s, were now developed into roller-blades — special boots with a built-in line of plastic wheels. And skateboards, which first appeared in the 1960s, were pushed to new extremes of speed and acrobatic skill.

The Virtual Future

What will electronic games be like in the future? They will probably respond to voice commands or interact with the human body. Headsets will create a lifelike imaginary world — a "virtual reality." Children will continue to enjoy

Home computer games have become more realistic.

games on the Internet, a worldwide computer communications system that already allows players a high level of interactivity.

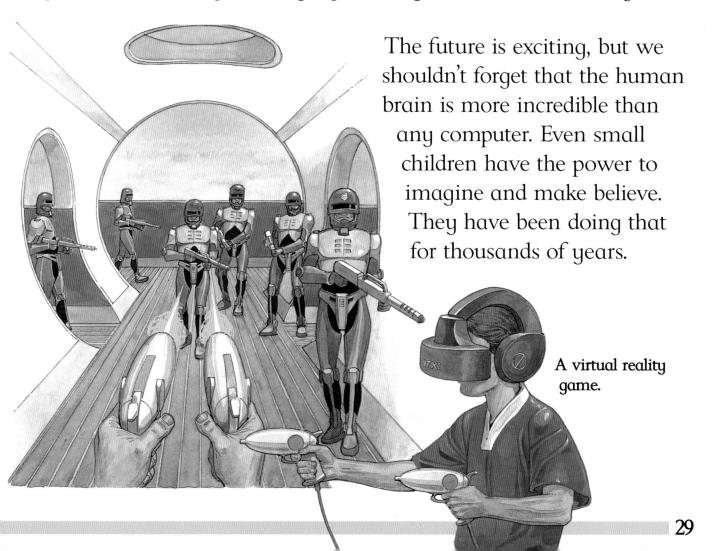

The future is exciting, but we shouldn't forget that the human brain is more incredible than any computer. Even small children have the power to imagine and make believe. They have been doing that for thousands of years.

A virtual reality game.

Time Line

B.C.

c. 2500	Sumerians play the royal board game in Ur.
c. 1300	A board game called senet is popular in Egypt.
c. 1000	Egyptian children play with toy lions.
c. 500	Greeks play with toy chariots.
c. 400	Greeks play with jointed clay dolls.
c. 300	Rag dolls, spinning tops, and balls are popular in Egypt.
	A game like soccer is played in China.

A.D.

300s	Roman children play with pull-along horses.
500	Chess invented in India.
c. 550	Mention of kites in China.
900s	Vikings play *hnefatafl*.
1100s	Checkers invented in France or Spain.
1300s	Pictures of toy windmills and battledore appear in England.
	Dolls of flat, baked clay are made in Germany.
	Playing cards reach Europe from Asia.
1413	Dolls being manufactured at Nuremberg, Germany.
1557	First known dollhouse made in Germany.
1560	Pieter Brueghel paints Children's Games.
1610	First known rocking horse made in England.
1746	A craze starts in France for pantins (jumping jacks).
1800	Wooden bricks and model building kits advertised in Nuremberg, Germany.
1811	Toy theaters appear in England.
1826	The first mechanical tin toys made by the Hess company, Nuremberg.
1842	Jumeau dolls made in Paris, France.
1853	The first velocipede, a model horse mounted on a tricycle.
1856	The first clockwork toys are manufactured in the United States.
1863	The first four-wheeled roller skates appear.
1866	Bru dolls made in Paris, France.
1903	First teddy bears manufactured, United States or Germany.
1907	The name Meccano is adopted by Frank Hornby for his metal model kits.
1930s	Toys linked to film characters, such as Mickey Mouse, appear.
1934	Danish toy maker Ole Kirk Christiansen calls his company Lego.
1958	Hula-hoop invented in the United States.
1959	First Barbie doll manufactured in the United States.
1972	First video game appears in the United States.
1975	First personal computer appears in the United States.
1990s	Virtual reality games and Internet become widely available.

Glossary

Backgammon An ancient game of dice and counters played over a two-part board.

Battledore (1) A simple version of badminton. (2) the bat used to play it.

Gourd The dried shell of a food plant, which can be turned into a rattle.

Marionette A puppet worked by strings.

Nine-men's-morris A board game in which the players try to line up nine counters on each side of a board marked out with four squares, one inside another.

Papier-mâché A material made from paper and glue that has been left to dry.

Papyrus A type of reed that grows on the banks of the River Nile, in North Africa. It was used by the ancient Egyptians to make paper and fabric.

Three-stones A Roman game called *terni lapilli*, in which one player had to prevent the other from lining up three pieces on the board.

Tinplate Thin sheet-iron coated with tin.

Velocipede (1) An early kind of bike or tricycle, (2) a model horse with wheels.

Victorian Dating from the reign of the British Queen Victoria (1837-1901).

Vikings People from the European region of Scandinavia, who attacked and settled in many other lands between about 1,200 and 900 years ago.

Further Reading

Doney, Meryl, *Games,* Franklin Watts, 1996

Erlbach, Arlene, *Teddy Bears,* Learner, 1997

Wardle, Susan, *Kites,* Putnam, 1996

Williams, John, *Toys and Games,* Raintree Steck-Vaughan, 1997

Index